**For MD & Zafolí,
Thanks for playing.**

"Children reproduce, transform, create and transmit culture through their own imaginative play, songs, dance, animation, stories, painting, games, street theatre, puppetry, festivals...

As they gain understanding of the cultural and artistic life around them from adult and peer relationships, they translate and adapt its meaning through their own generational experience.

Through engagement with their peers, children create and transmit their own language, games, secret worlds, fantasies and other cultural knowledge."

United Nations Convention on the Rights of the Child (UNCRC)

The Persian Alphabet

We want to simplify your Persian learning journey as it is such a unique & enigmatic language. There are 32 official Persian letters. The letters change form depending on their position in a word or when they appear separate from other letters. For example, the letter ghayn غ has four ways of being written depending on where it appears in any given word:

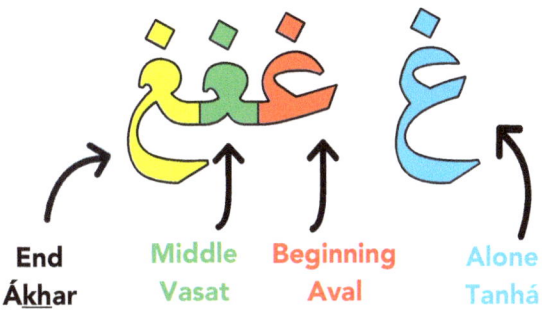

End
Ákhar

Middle
Vasat

Beginning
Aval

Alone
Tanhá

It is important to note that Persian books are read from right to left (←). There are 7 separate/stand-alone letters that do not connect in the same way to adjacent letters (these will be depicted in blue). They are:

Stand alone
Tanhá vámístan

The short vowels a, e & o are usually omitted in literature and are depicted by markings above & below letters (ـَـ). They are not allocated a letter name, unlike their long vowel counterparts á: alef, í: ye & ú: váv (و ی آ).

Pronunciation Guide©

Persian	English	Pronunciation
اَ	a	**a**nt
آ	á	**a**rm
ب	b	**b**at
د	d	**d**og
اِ	e	**e**nd
ف	f	**f**un
گ	g	**g**o
ه	h	**h**at
ح	h	**h**at
ی	í	m**ee**t
ج	j	**j**et
ک	k	**k**ey
ل	l	**l**ove
م	m	**m**e
ن	n	**n**ap
اُ	o	**o**n
پ	p	**p**at
ق	q/gh*	me**r**ci
ر	r	**r**un
س	s	**s**un
ص	s	**s**un
ث	s	**s**un

Persian	English	Pronunciation
ت	t	**t**op
ط	t	**t**op
و	ú	m**oo**n
و	v	**v**an
ی	y	**y**es
ذ	z	**z**oo
ز	z	**z**oo
ض	z	**z**oo
ظ	z	**z**oo
چ	ch	**ch**air
غ	gh*	me**r**ci
خ	kh*	ba**ch**
ش	sh	**sh**are
ژ	zh	plea**s**ure
ع	'	uh-oh†

*	guttural sound from back of throat
†	glottal stop, breathing pause
ّ	double letter
ً	letter 'n' sound
لا	combination of letter l & á (lá)
ای	long í sound (ee in m**ee**t)
اِی	long í sound (ee in m**ee**t)
(...)	colloquial use

This book was inspired by my crazy Persian family and the games I played growing up as part of the Iranian diaspora in Australia. Games that my mámán [mum] and bábá [dad] taught me. Games I beat my brothers playing.☺

Playing games is not only fun, but it can also help establish deep and meaningful bonds. It can also teach the following skills:
problem solving 🧠, strategy ♟, numeracy ①,
high frequency words 🔡, hand eye coordination 👁, team building 💝,
fine motor skills 🖐, gross motor skills 🚶, memory 👂,
cultural & familial connection 🏩 through play.
Bonding with our children while learning about our unique and wonderful heritage.

Baráye bozorg va kúchúlú.

قایِم موشَک

Number of People: Minimum 2
Aim of the game:
Hide for the longest time before being found.

How to play: One child (the detective) closes their eyes (no peeking) and counts to 10, the other children go to find hiding spots. When finished counting, the detective needs to find all the children.

Sok sok version:
The location of where the detective starts counting is called the base camp. If the detective leaves base camp to look for children. The children that are hiding can approach base camp can yell: "sok sok" and touch/tag the space before the detective returns. Anyone who returns to base camp and calls "Sok sok" before the detective, wins the game.

Skills developed:
strategy ♟ , numeracy ❶ , gross motor skills 🚶 , team building ♥

Hide and Seek

Gháyem mús̲h̲ak

قایِم موشَک

á: as (a) in arm
ú: as (oo) in moon

تَختِه نَرد

Number of People: 2

Aim of the game: Move all your checkers into the home side of your board and then remove them completely.

How to play: Each player has 15 coloured checkers. Setting them up at specific points on the board (2 placed at 24-point, 3 at 8-point, 5 at 13-point and 5 at 6-point). Each player rolls one dice and the player with the highest number starts. To move the checkers each player rolls both dice. Players must move their checkers according to the numbers on each dice (eg if the player rolls 4 and 3, then they must move one checker 4 moves and another checker 3 moves). First to remove all checkers from the board, wins.

Skills developed:
strategy♟, problem solving🧩, Numeracy➊,
cultural & familial connection 🖼, fine motor skills✋

Backgammon

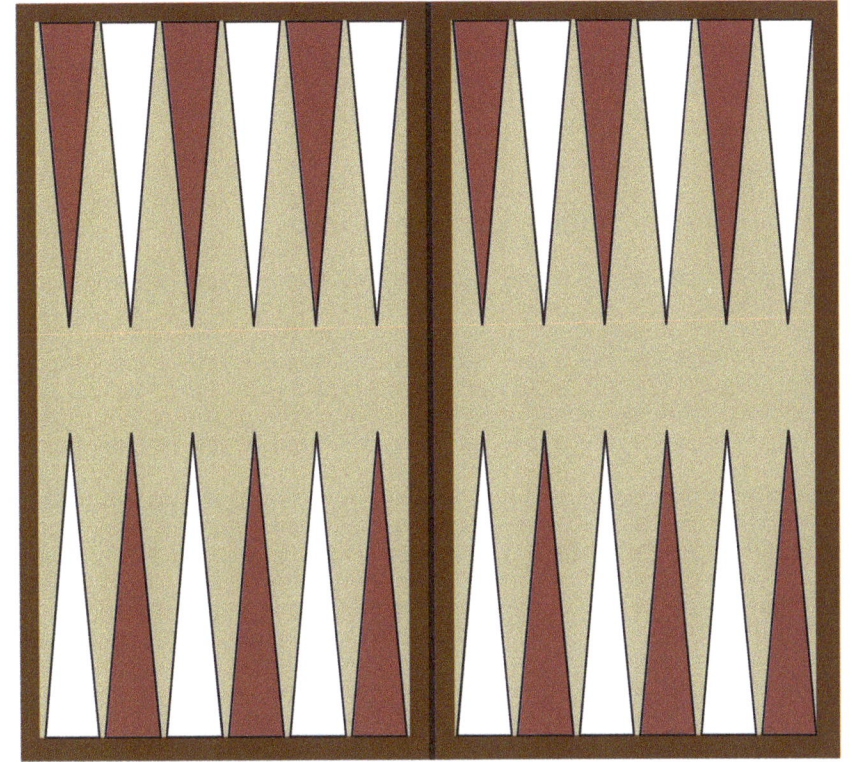

Takhteh nard

تَختِه نَرد

بازی لی لی

Number of People: 1 - 10

Aim of the game:
Move across the floor by jumping into particular squares.

How to play:
Use chalk/other drawing medium to map out numbers on the floor in square boxes. Find a rock/coin and throw on the numbers in sequential order. Whichever number the rock lands on, you can't jump into that square and must hop over that box to finish the game.

Skills developed:
Numeracy❶, hand eye co-ordination◉, gross motor skills 🚶.

Hopscotch

Bází ley ley
بازی لی لی

á: as (a) in <u>a</u>rm
í: as (ee) in m<u>ee</u>t

شَطرَنج

Number of People: 2

Aim of the game:
Capture and destroy the oppositions king [shah]

Pieces:
Pawn : sarbáz : سَرباز
Bishop : fíl : فیل
Knight : asb : اسب
Rook : ru<u>kh</u> : روخ
Queen / counsellor : vazír : وَزیر
King : <u>Sh</u>ah : شاه

Skills developed:
strategy, problem solving, Numeracy, high frequency words, fine motor skills

Chess

<u>s</u>hatranj

شَطرَنج

پاسور

Number of People: 2 - 4

Aim of the game: Be the first player to reach 62 points.

How to play: A fishing game where the cards are matched & collected by their numerical value to the value of 11.
Value of each numerical card according to the number of the card (A:1, 2:2 etc). A Queen (Q) can only be collected by a Q, a King (K) with a K. A Jack (J) can collect all the cards on the deck (except Q & K's). Point system: A:1, J:1, >7 Clubs:7 [haft kháj] ♣, 10 diamonds:3 ♦, Súr:5
Súr: If you collect all cards on the table leaving no cards on the table you gain a súr.

Each of the players adds their points to their cumulative total for the game. The first player to reach 62 or more points is the winner.

Skills developed:
Numeracy❶, strategy 👥, problem solving 🧠
high frequency words🔠, fine motor skills✍

Cards

Pásúr

پاسور

[Haft kháj, Yázdahtáyí, Cháhár barg]

á: as (a) in arm
ú: as (oo) in moon
í: as (ee) in meet

Number of People: 2 - 4

Aim of the game:
Be the first team to win 7 rounds.

How to play: The person who gets the first Ace gets to pick the 'hokm' or the 'trump' suit, they are called Hákem (ruler/governor). Dealer deals 13 cards to each player. Starting with 5 cards to the Hákem, who picks the Hokm suit based on what they are dealt. Card values: highest A, K, Q, J, 10, 9, 8, 7, 6, 5, 4, 3, 2 lowest

The hákem starts the game by playing the first card. Other players must play cards from the same suit (the highest card value wins the round). If the player doesn't have that suit they can use a 'trump' card to win that round (what's termed 'cut'). By cutting the suit with the hokm suit the team wins the round.

Skills developed:
Numeracy❶, strategy ⚄, problem solving 🗣
high frequency words🎹, fine motor skills✍

Trump Card Game

Hokm

غاب بازی

Number of People: 2 - 6

Aim of the game: Catch the most pebbles in your hand after throwing them in the air without dropping them.

How to play:
Each child takes it in turns to throw the pebbles into the air and tries to catch them on the back of their hands. Then flips their hand back to try and capture as many pebbles as possible in the inner palm of their hands. After each round an additional pebble is added.

"Ye *qol*" (one flower) is when one pebble is thrown up and the remaining four are collected one by one; *do-qol* when one pebble is thrown up and two pebbles at a time are collected and more.

Skills developed:
Numeracy❶, strategy ♟, problem solving 🧠
high frequency words🎹, fine motor skills✋

Knucklebones/jax

Gháb bází/ye ghol do ghol

غاب بازی

á: as (a) in arm
í: as (ee) in meet

وَسَطى

Number of People: 3 – no maximum

Aim of the game: to not get hit with the ball and to catch the ball without ball bouncing on the ground.

How to play:
Children divided into even numbers in two groups (can be played with one child in the middle if only 3 players). Children on either side have to try and throw the ball to 'tag' those in the middle without letting them catch the ball. When tagged you are out. If you catch the ball without it bouncing you get to bring back one of the previously tagged players. Each team has ten tries to tag the other team out.

Skills developed:
Numeracy❶, hand eye co-ordination◉ and gross motor skills 𝄅.

Piggy in the middle

vasatí

وَسَطى

í: as (ee) in m<u>ee</u>t

كُشتی

Number of People: 2- 10

Aim of the game: Pin down your children/parent onto the ground for 10 seconds counting when both shoulders are square on the floor. This is best played on a soft floor mat/thick carpet. Usually its parent vs child/children to help children bond and work together to bring down the parent.

How to play:
Children try to pin down the parent/s for 10secs with back & shoulders on the ground. If shoulder/back no longer on the floor you must stop counting. 1st person to pin down opponent for 10secs, wins.

Skills developed:
gross motor skills 🚶, Numeracy❶, team building♥

Note: This is more of a laugh and tumble game played on soft mats- not a serious showdown where people get hurt. We do not condone violence towards anyone. This game should only be played with full consent. The tone must be a joyful and fun.

Wrestling

koshtí
کُشتی

í: as (ee) in m<u>ee</u>t

Number of People: 2 - 10

Aim of the game:
To try and name objects that can fly so fast that you can trick others into moving their hands up when non-flying objects are named.

How to play:
Take it in turns to say the names of flying objects
(usually birds but can be other flying objects like aeroplanes)
Go around faster and faster and move your hand up from ground to above your head when each person states an item/object. Whoever moves their hand up when a nonflying object is named loses that round.

Skills gained:
strategy ⛨, numeracy ❶, high frequency words ▦,
🧠 hand eye coordination 👁, memory 👄,

Sparrow fly

gonjeshk par

Crow : Kalá<u>gh</u> : كلاغ
Magpie : zá<u>gh</u>y : زاغی
Sparrow : gonje<u>sh</u>k : گنجشک
Pidgeon : kabútar : کبوتر
Dove : kabútar : کبوتر
Eagle : o'<u>gh</u>áb : عقاب
Owl : jo<u>gh</u>d : جغد

گُلیا پوچ

Number of People: 2 – no maximum

Aim of the game:
Hide object in hand so that it is well hidden.

How to play:
One person places small paper/stone/coin/tissue in palm of hand. Once they have hidden the object in their fist they show both fists to onlookers (they can hide behind their backs or switch item in hands). The person who guesses the correct hand object is located in gets to hide object in their hand and the game continues. If they fail to guess correct hand original person can hide item again until they guess correctly.

Skills gained:
strategy ♟, high frequency words 🔡,
hand eye coordination 👁, memory 🧠

Golíá pú<u>ch</u>

Golíá pú<u>ch</u>

í: as (ee) in m<u>ee</u>t
á: as (a) in <u>a</u>rm
ú: as (oo) in m<u>oo</u>n

Number of People: 2

How to play:
Draw little circles around the palm of your childs hand and sing
"lili lili hozak, jújeh omad áb bokhoreh oftád túyeh hozak."
As you read this part, close each finger into the palm of the hand to make a fist.

As you open each finger you say...
First finger "ín yeki daresh ávord"
Second finger 'Ín yeki ábesh dád"
Third finger "in yeki núnesh dád
Fourth Finger Kí holesh dád?
Thumb "in yeki goft: maneh maneh kaleh gondeh!"

Skills gained:
high frequency words, memory
high frequency words, fine motor skills

lílí lílí hozak

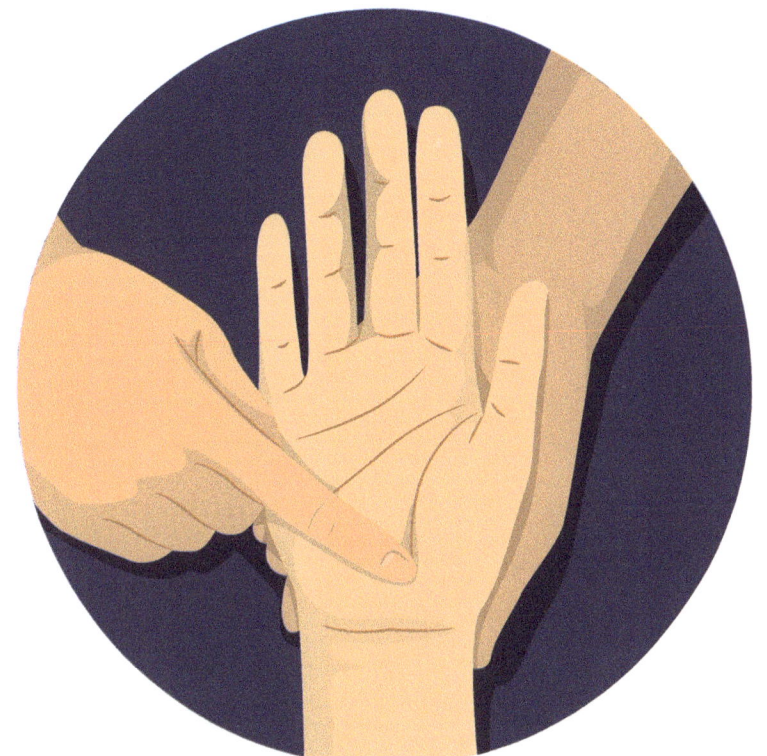

Lílí lílí hozak

لیلی لیلی هُزَک

í:　as (ee) in m<u>ee</u>t

عَتَل مَتَل توتولِه

Number of People: 2

How to play:
Line up all the children who wish to play with their legs lined up next to each other. Tap each leg with each syllable of the song:

Atal matal tútúle
Gáveh hasan che júreh
Na shír dare na pestún
Shíresho bordan hendestún
Yeh zane kordí bestún
Esmesho bezár a'mqází
Doreh kolásh ghermezí
Hachín o váchín Ye pá to varchín

If the song ends on a child's leg then that leg is folded and can no longer count in the game. Last person with a leg in the game, wins.

Skills gained:
numeracy ❶, high frequency words 🎛, hand eye coordination 👁, memory 🧠, gross motor skills 🚶

atal matal

Atal matal túlúleh

عَتَل مَتَل توتولِه

ú: as (oo) in m<u>oo</u>n

نون بيار كباب بيار

Number of People: 2

Aim of the game:
To 'burn' the opponents hand by slapping them before they move their hand from the 'grill'.

How to play:
Children face each other with their hands out. One child's hands below (grill), and one child's hand placed ontop of the other child's hand (nún/kabáb). The hands below need to try and slap the hands above before they move them away.

Skills gained:
strategy ♟, hand eye coordination 👁, gross motor skills 🚶

Bring bread, Take the kabáb

Nún bíár kabáb bebar
نون بیار کباب بیار

ú: as (oo) in m<u>oo</u>n
í: as (ee) in m<u>ee</u>t
á: as (a) in <u>a</u>rm

تیله بازی

Number of People: 2 - 4

Aim of the game:
To win as many marbles as possible.
Person with the most marbles at the end, wins.

How to play:
Dig a small hole and place your marble close to it. The opponent must put his marble on the ground and try to hit the opponents marble or get his marble into the opposing hole (<u>kh</u>úneh) by shooting his marble with his fingers. If your marbles are hit they are taken by the opponent. Person with the most marbles at the end, wins.

Skills gained:
strategy ♟, numeracy ❶, hand eye coordination 👁, gross motor skills 🚶, gross motor skills 🚶

Marbles

Tíleh bází

تیله بازی

í: as (ee) in m<u>ee</u>t
á: as (a) in <u>a</u>rm

www.ingramcontent.com/pod-product-compliance
Lightning Source LLC
Chambersburg PA
CBHW061135010526
44107CB00068B/2944